THE
CAROLS
WE LOVE

Daniel Partner

BARBOUR
PUBLISHING

© 2002 by Barbour Publishing, Inc.

ISBN 1-58660-741-3

Cover image © Adobe Studios

Scripture quotations are taken from the King James Version of the Bible.

Published by Barbour Publishing, Inc., P.O. Box 719, Uhrichsville, OH 44683, www.barbourbooks.com

Previously published as *Sounds of the Season.*

Our mission is to publish and distribute inspirational products offering exceptional value and biblical encouragement to the masses.

 Member of the
Evangelical Christian
Publishers Association

Printed in the United States of America.
5 4 3 2 1

THE
CAROLS
WE LOVE

INTRODUCTION

All around the world, regardless of their age, nationality, or status in life, people love Christmas. For some, the pleasure comes from gifts and parties. For others, it's the deeper realization that God's own Son, Jesus Christ, was born in a stable in Bethlehem to become the way of salvation for humanity.

But for almost everyone, there's something special about the music of Christmas—those wonderful songs, ancient and contemporary, that spread the same "good tidings of great joy" that angels shared with the awed shepherds of Judaea so many years ago.

This book focuses on twenty-two of the most powerful songs of Christmas. In these pages, you'll find the lyrics for each song and read about its history, meaning, or implications.

If you get to know your favorite Christmas songs better, you may know the Christ of the Christmas songs better, too. And you'll enjoy *The Carols We Love* even more!

We Three Kings

We three kings of Orient are;
Bearing gifts, we traverse afar,
Field and fountain, moor and mountain,
Following yonder star.

Refrain
   O star of wonder, star of light,
   Star with royal beauty bright,
   Westward leading, still proceeding,
   Guide us to thy perfect light.

Born a King on Bethlehem's plain
Gold I bring to crown Him again,
King forever, ceasing never,
Over us all to reign.

Refrain

Frankincense to offer have I;
Incense owns a Deity nigh;
Prayer and praising, voices raising,
Worshipping God on high.

Refrain

Myrrh is mine, its bitter perfume
Breathes a life of gathering gloom;
Sorrowing, sighing, bleeding, dying,
Sealed in the stone cold tomb.

Refrain

Glorious now behold Him arise;
King and God and sacrifice;
Alleluia, Alleluia,
Sounds through the earth and skies.

Refrain

JOHN HENRY HOPKINS, JR. 1820–1891

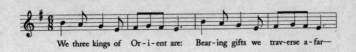
We three kings of Or-i-ent are: Bear-ing gifts we trav-erse a-far—

Now when Jesus was born in Bethlehem of Judaea
in the days of Herod the king, behold,
there came wise men from the east to Jerusalem,
Saying, Where is he that is born King of the Jews?
for we have seen his star in the east,
and are come to worship him.
MATTHEW 2:1–2

The story of the wise men who visited Jesus and His parents is a mystery. A star led to their arrival, and a dream warned them to depart. No one knows who they were, where exactly they came from, or how many there were; astronomers and historians cannot positively identify the star they followed; and it is unclear when they arrived in Bethlehem. But these things are not really important. The story is not about the so-called "three kings." The meaning of the story is found in the wise men's three gifts.

"And when they had opened their treasures, they presented unto him gifts; gold, and frankincense, and myrrh" (Matthew 2:11). Each gift is quite valuable. Scholars guess that the sale of these items financed the family's retreat to Egypt as they fled from the wrath of

Herod (verse 13). But the three gifts are also richly prophetic—they symbolize who and what the child Jesus would be.

One verse of this song is devoted to each gift. Gold was the treasure of kings—Jesus was born to be King of the Jews. The burning of frankincense was an important part of ancient Israel's worship of God. This gift indicates that the child, Jesus, was God. Myrrh, a spice used to embalm the dead, predicted Christ's death to be Savior of the world.

The final verse gives the tally of the life of the babe of Bethlehem and the proper sum of our response to Him:

Glorious now behold Him arise,
King and God and sacrifice;
Alleluia, alleluia!
Earth to heaven replies.

Hark! The Herald Angels Sing

Hark! The herald angels sing,
"Glory to the newborn King;
Peace on earth, and mercy mild,
God and sinners reconciled!"
Joyful, all ye nations rise,
Join the triumph of the skies;
With th'angelic host proclaim,
"Christ is born in Bethlehem!"

Refrain

Hark! the herald angels sing,
"Glory to the newborn King!"

CHARLES WESLEY, 1707–1788

Hark! the her - ald an - gels sing, "Glo - ry to the new-born King;

As the apple tree among the trees of the wood,
so is my beloved among the sons.
I sat down under his shadow
with great delight,
and his fruit was sweet to my taste.
He brought me to the banqueting house,
and his banner over me was love.
SONG OF SOLOMON 2:3–4

This hymn was written by Charles Wesley, brother to John Wesley, and one of the most prolific of all hymn writers. The Wesleys founded the Methodist movement in England in the mid-eighteenth century. They utilized hymns not only to direct worshipers' hearts to God, but also to teach the truth of the gospel. "Hark! The Herald Angels Sing" helps answer the questions, "Who is Jesus Christ?" and "Why was He born?"

The first verse announces that Jesus came to reconcile God with humanity. In the next verse, the newborn child, Jesus, is the incarnate Deity—God come in the flesh. The last verse gives three reasons Christ was born—that man would not die, to bring resurrection into humanity, and to make available the second birth.

It also tells of three things He brought with Him—healing, light, and life.

Several titles of Jesus appear in the hymn—King, Lord, Emmanuel (which means "God with us"), Prince of Peace, and Sun of Righteousness. These tell us not only who He is, but what He does: The King leads a kingdom, the Lord accepts worship, Emmanuel provides companionship, and the Sun offers warmth and light for the growth of righteousness.

How attractive He is! Jesus Christ is the true beauty of Christmas.

DEAR LORD,
I ASK YOU FOR ONLY ONE
CHRISTMAS GIFT—
THAT I WOULD SEE YOU
AND KNOW YOUR LOVE.

Angels We Have Heard on High

Angels we have heard on high
Sweetly singing o'er the plains,
And the mountains in reply
Echoing their joyous strains.

Refrain

> *Gloria, in excelsis Deo!*
> *Gloria, in excelsis Deo!*

Shepherds, why this jubilee?
Why your joyous strains prolong?
What the gladsome tidings be
Which inspire your heavenly song?

Refrain

Come to Bethlehem and see
Christ Whose birth the angels sing;
Come, adore on bended knee,
Christ the Lord, the newborn King.

Refrain

See Him in a manger laid,
Whom the choirs of angels praise;
Mary, Joseph, lend your aid,
While our hearts in love we raise.

Refrain

FRENCH CAROL, 18TH CENTURY

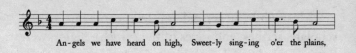

An-gels we have heard on high, Sweet-ly sing-ing o'er the plains,

And looking upon Jesus
as he walked, he saith,
Behold the Lamb of God!
JOHN 1:36

The bright French carol "Les Anges dans Nos Campagnes" was first published, text and tune, in *Nouveau Recueil de Cantiques* (1855). Soon, in 1862, James Chadwick (1813–1882) translated and published it in English.

"Angels We Have Heard on High," probably the best known of all the traditional French carols, tells of the angelic announcement of Jesus' birth to shepherds in a field near Bethlehem. Who would have expected this? God sent the herald angels to simple shepherds!

Scholars think that these shepherds may have been those who supplied lambs for sacrifice at the temple in nearby Jerusalem. There, for generations, the God of Abraham, Isaac, and Jacob had been worshiped. The most important ceremony was the yearly sacrifice of a lamb for the forgiveness of sin. But on this night, the shepherds were called away from their duty to greet the true Lamb of God.

15

Meanwhile, in Jerusalem, the preeminent priests, scholars, scribes, and sages of the Jewish religion were not informed of Christ's birth. God did not tell them that the crowning glory of Israel had arrived. He came to Earth in an unexpected, secretive way. About thirty-three years later, this unknown newborn, Jesus Christ, would make the final sacrifice and take away the sins of the whole world once and for all with His death on the hill called Golgotha.

O God of the Lord Jesus Christ,
Father of glory,
give me a spirit of wisdom
and revelation
as I come to know the Son.

Go, Tell It on the Mountain

Refrain

Go, tell it on the mountain,
Over the hills and everywhere
Go, tell it on the mountain,
That Jesus Christ is born.

While shepherds kept their watching
Over silent flocks by night
Behold throughout the heavens
There shone a holy light.

JOHN W. WORK, JR., 1872–1925

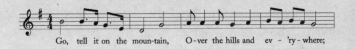

Go, tell it on the moun-tain,   O-ver the hills and   ev - 'ry-where;

O Zion, that bringest good tidings,
get thee up into the high mountain;
O Jerusalem, that bringest good tidings,
lift up thy voice with strength;
lift it up, be not afraid;
say unto the cities of Judah,
Behold your God!
ISAIAH 40:9

Six months after the end of the Civil War, an institution of learning was founded in a former Union army barracks in Nashville, Tennessee. Classes were convened on January 9, 1866, for students ranging in age from seven to seventy. Their background was slavery and poverty. They were thirsty for education.

The founders wanted their school to be open to all, regardless of race. It would measure itself by "the highest standards, not of Negro education, but of American education at its best." They incorporated Fisk University on August 22, 1867.

The world-famous Jubilee Singers originated as a group of Fisk University students who began traveling in 1871, praying that through their music they could raise enough money to keep the doors of their debt-ridden school open. Before long, their performances were electrifying audiences throughout the United States and Europe. The Jubilee Singers introduced much of the world to the spiritual as a musical genre—and in the process raised the funds that preserved their school.

At Fisk, John Wesley Work, Jr. (1871–1925), an alumnus and faculty member, was a leader in the movement to preserve, study, and perform Negro spirituals. He trained and performed with the professional and student groups of the Jubilee Singers, and collected, harmonized, and published a number of collections of slave songs and spirituals. In 1907, Work wrote the lyrics to "Go, Tell It on the Mountain" and set them to the tune of the old spiritual "When I Was a Seeker." It is a rare and wonderful Christmas song that has sprung from the rich tradition of African-American music.

Lord Jesus,
I ask that the world
would know You;
that on the mountain
or in the valley,
people would see and hear,
and most of all,
enjoy the unsearchable riches
of Christ.

It Came Upon the Midnight Clear

It came upon the midnight clear,
　　that glorious song of old,
From angels bending near the earth,
　　to touch their harps of gold;
"Peace on the earth, good will to men,
　　from heaven's all gracious King."
The world in solemn stillness lay,
　　to hear the angels sing.

EDMUND H. SEARS, 1810–1876

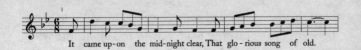

It came up-on the mid-night clear, That glo-rious song of old.

So then faith cometh by hearing,
and hearing by the word of God.
ROMANS 10:17

By 1849, the Industrial Revolution had fully arrived in New England. Farmers and their families left the stony soil of the homeplace, moved to better lands in the west, or entered the mills and factories to endure, alone, long days of relentless labor. This was the year Edmund Hamilton Sears, a minister in Wayland, Massachusetts, published his great hymn, "It Came Upon a Midnight Clear," in the *Christian Register*.

Sears's song reflects the social upheaval wreaked by the Industrial Revolution. It begins beautifully— "It came upon a midnight clear/That glorious song of old"—but for the many tens of thousands of people who underwent the overthrow of the old agrarian ways, midnight was still upon the earth. And sadly, a mere twelve years after churches began to sing the angel's greeting—"Peace on the earth, good will to men/From heav'n's all gracious King"—the American Civil War ripped viciously through the land.

The hymn does not offer a view of the world

through rose-colored glasses. Speaking directly to those "beneath life's crushing load. . .who toil along the way," it delivers this appeal: "hush the noise, ye men of strife, and hear the angels sing."

This is not asking too much: Simply listen—"And the angel said unto them, Fear not: for, behold, I bring you good tidings of great joy, which shall be to all people. For unto you is born this day in the city of David a Saviour, which is Christ the Lord" (Luke 2:10–11). This hymn makes a modest request to all people: In the Christmas season, "rest beside the weary road/And hear the angels sing."

HEAVENLY FATHER, IN THIS SEASON
OF EATING AND DRINKING
AND GIVING OF PRETTY GIFTS,
OPEN SOME HEARTS TO A GLIMPSE
OF WHAT YOU HAVE PREPARED
FOR THOSE WHO LOVE YOU.

O Little Town of Bethlehem

O little town of Bethlehem,
    how still we see thee lie!
Above thy deep and dreamless sleep
    the silent stars go by.
Yet in thy dark streets shineth
    the everlasting Light;
The hopes and fears of all the years
    are met in thee tonight.

PHILLIPS BROOKS, 1835–1893

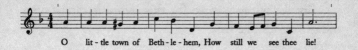

O lit - tle town of Beth - le - hem, How still we see thee lie!

Marvel not that I said unto thee,
Ye must be born again.
The wind bloweth where it listeth,
and thou hearest the sound thereof,
but canst not tell whence it
cometh, and whither it goeth:
so is every one that is born of the Spirit.
JOHN 3:7–8

Phillips Brooks (1835–1893), minister of Holy Trinity Episcopal Church, Philadelphia, wrote this hymn in 1868. Three years earlier, he had been in the Holy Land at Christmastime. His hymn recalls the peaceful view of nineteenth-century Bethlehem from the hills of Palestine at night. It marvels that in the dark and quiet beauty of this little town, long ago, the Everlasting Light was born. "While mortals sleep," intones the song, "the angels keep their watch" over the Christ child. And even more wondrous is the silent, even secret way in which the Savior came into this world. "So God imparts to human hearts/The blessings of His heaven."

27

Brooks wrote a verse for this hymn is rarely sung today. It goes like this:

> Where children pure and happy
> Pray to the blessed child,
> Where misery cries out to thee,
> Son of the mother mild;
> Where charity stands watching
> And faith holds wide the door,
> The dark night wakes, the glory breaks,
> And Christmas comes once more.

Christmas can be a nostalgic time of recalling the past, even the far distant days of Christ's birth. But Phillips Brooks says that Christmas can come once more in a human heart. How can this happen? Can it happen to you? Yes, if you pray the prayer of the hymn's final verse: "O holy child of Bethlehem! Descend to me, I pray; cast out my sin and enter in, be born in me today."

LORD JESUS,
I BELIEVE THAT YOU HEAR
MY PRAYER.

O Come, O Come, Emmanuel

O come, O come, Emmanuel,
And ransom captive Israel,
That mourns in lonely exile here
Until the Son of God appear.

Refrain

Rejoice! Rejoice!
Emmanuel shall come to thee, O Israel.

LATIN HYMN

O come, O come, Em-man - u - el, And ran-som cap-tive

We have also a more sure word of prophecy;
whereunto ye do well that ye take heed,
as unto a light that shineth in a dark place,
until the day dawn,
and the day star arise in your hearts.

2 PETER 1:19

First written in Latin in the twelfth century, this song was sung in monasteries during vespers, one of the seven services held on seven consecutive days during Advent. The carol prays for the advent of Christ, calling upon Him in five verses using five names. Each name embodies and represents one aspect of Christ.

The carol first prays for the advent, or the appearance, of Emmanuel, a name meaning "God with us."

Therefore the Lord himself
shall give you a sign; Behold,
a virgin shall conceive, and bear a son,
and shall call his name Immanuel.

ISAIAH 7:14

Advent means "coming." The baby who was born in

Bethlehem was the coming of the Lord of might who gave the law to Israel at Sinai.

For unto us a child is born. . .and his name
shall be called. . .The mighty God.
ISAIAH 9:6

Advent also means "arrival." The song calls Jesus "the rod of Jessie." He arrived like the shoot of a new tree that comes out of an old stump.

And there shall come forth a rod out of the stem of Jesse.
ISAIAH 11:1

Advent also signifies an approach. Christ is the dayspring, the dawn of the approaching eternal day.

Through the tender mercy of our God;
whereby the dayspring from on high hath visited us.
LUKE 1:78

Finally, advent means "drawing near." The song prays, "O come thou key of David, come/And open wide our heavenly home." As the kingdom of God draws near, He is our key to eternal life.

And the key of the house of David
will I lay upon his shoulder;
so he shall open, and none shall shut.
ISAIAH 22:22

JESUS CHRIST,
I PRAY YOU WILL COME AGAIN.
BREAK UPON US LIKE THE DAWN
AND UNLOCK THE KINGDOM OF GOD
ON THIS EARTH FOREVER.

The First Noel

The first Noel the angel did say
Was to certain poor shepherds in fields as
    they lay;
In fields where they lay tending their sheep,
On a cold winter's night that was so deep.

Refrain

Noel, Noel, Noel, Noel,
Born is the King of Israel.

Traditional English Carol

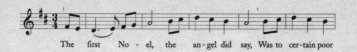

The first No - el, the an-gel did say, Was to cer-tain poor

For unto you is born this day
in the city of David a Saviour,
which is Christ the Lord.
LUKE 2:11

This traditional English Christmas carol dates from the fourteenth century—the early dawn of the Renaissance. In those days, after centuries of religious repression, people had begun to dance again. To "carol" originally meant to dance a carol. These were festive circle dances accompanied by singing. So later, "carol" meant both to sing and dance a carol. Eventually, to "carol" meant merely to sing a carol.

Did you ever wonder what a *Noël* is and why the word appears only at Christmastime? Noël means *birth*. The English borrowed the word from the French, who adapted it from Latin. Noël is always capitalized because it signifies one particular birth—that of Jesus Christ. And so we sing this ancient, festive carol about the first Noël.

Human history includes untold billions of births. But the refrain of this old carol recognizes only one. When singing *Noël, Noël, Noël, Noël,* we proclaim:

Birth, Birth, Birth, Birth,
The King of Israel has been born!

The birth of Jesus—it was the incarnation of God, the entrance of the Creator into the creation. What a birth this is! It is indeed one-of-a-kind and so deserves a word to be reserved for it only. Noël!

The gospel describes the Noël like this:

> *In the beginning was the Word,*
> *and the Word was with God,*
> *and the Word was God.*
> *And the Word was made flesh,*
> *and dwelt among us,*
> *(and we beheld his glory, the glory*
> *as of the only begotten of the Father,)*
> *full of grace and truth.*
> *And of his fulness have all we received,*
> *and grace for grace.*
> JOHN 1:1, 14, 16

This is something to celebrate every day—Noël, Noël, Noël, Noël!

Lord Jesus,
I ask in this seasonal
celebration of Your birth that
my eyes will see Your salvation, which You
have prepared
for everyone. Let it be a light
for revelation to the nations
and for glory to Your people Israel.

Away in a Manger

Away in a manger, no crib for a bed,
The little Lord Jesus laid down His sweet head.
The stars in the sky looked down where He lay,
The little Lord Jesus, asleep on the hay.

ST. 1, 2, ANONYMOUS, 1885

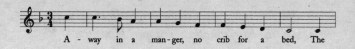

A - way in a man-ger, no crib for a bed, The

And this shall be a sign unto you;
Ye shall find the babe
wrapped in swaddling clothes,
lying in a manger.
LUKE 2:12

This lovely children's carol probably has its source in the German-American community of the nineteenth century. It first appeared in *Little Children's Book for Schools and Families* (1885), published by the Evangelical Lutheran Church in North America, and J. R. Murray's *Dainty Songs for Little Lads and Lasses* (1887). It is likely that Murray composed the tune, but he attributed the carol to Martin Luther, calling it "Luther's Cradle Hymn."

The song tells a little children's story with a lovely prayer at the end. The story goes like this:

On a night far away, and long ago, a baby boy was born. His mother and father had no crib for Him that night. But in a nearby barn was a feed trough, where farm animals ate their daily grain. The trough was almost the same size as a cradle. So, as the stars shone bright in the sky above, the baby's mother wrapped Him in a warm blanket and laid Him in the feed trough where He fell asleep on a cushion of hay.

Soon, as the sun was brightening the morning sky, the farm animals began to stir. A rooster called: "cock-a-doodle-do!" A cow began to softly moo. She was ready to be milked. The newborn baby awoke, His mother gathered Him close in her arms to still His crying, and so the life of Jesus Christ began.

I love Thee, Lord Jesus.
Look down from the sky
and stay by my cradle
'til morning is nigh.

What Child Is This?

What Child is this, who, laid to rest
On Mary's lap is sleeping?
Whom angels greet with anthems sweet,
While shepherds watch are keeping?
This, this is Christ the King,
Whom shepherds guard and angels sing;
Haste, haste, to bring Him laud,
The Babe, the Son of Mary.

WILLIAM C. DIX, 1827–1898

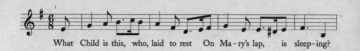

What Child is this, who, laid to rest   On Ma - ry's lap,   is sleep-ing?

> *And he hath put a new song in my mouth,*
> *even praise unto our God.*
> PSALM 40:3

Each year the songs of Christmas are heard everywhere. Where did they all come from? Naturally, they arise from many sources. But, generally, it is safe to say that the songs of Christmas arose from hearts of people who love Jesus Christ.

This pretty carol first appeared in *Christmas Carols New and Old* (1867). It was written by William Chatterton Dix (1837–1898), who was educated in the Grammar School of Bristol in preparation for a commercial career. After school, he became the manager of a marine insurance company in Glasgow, a vocation which he followed to the end of his life.

His father, a surgeon, had a gift for poetry and wrote "The Life of Thomas Chatterton," about a minor English poet. So William Chatterton Dix inherited a true gift for writing verse, especially hymns. Dix wrote many Christmas and Easter carols, but the most widely known is "What Child Is This?" written in about 1865 and set to the traditional folk melody "Greensleeves."

William Dix published more than forty hymns, including "Alleluia! Sing to Jesus!" "As with Gladness, Men of Old," "Come unto Me, Ye Weary," "Joy Fills Our Inmost Hearts Today!" "O Thou, the Eternal Son of God," and "To Thee, O Lord, Our Hearts We Raise." But he is probably best remembered for his contribution to our carols of Christmas.

Thank You, God,
for the gift of song.
And thank You for the lives
of the people
through whom You operated
to bring the sounds
of this Christmas season
to my ears.

Bring a Torch, Jeanette, Isabella

Bring a torch, Jeanette, Isabella,
Bring a torch, come swiftly and run.
Christ is born, tell the folk of the village,
Jesus is sleeping in His cradle,
Ah, ah, beautiful is the Mother,
Ah, ah, beautiful is her Son.

Traditional

Bring a torch Jean-ette Is-a-bel-la, Bring a

And she brought forth her firstborn son,
and wrapped him in swaddling clothes,
and laid him in a manger;
because there was no room
for them in the inn.
LUKE 2:7

The popularity of carols began during the Renaissance. They were often English songs of religious joy associated with Christmas, though "carol" is a medieval word that could mean a variety of things—a popular dance song, a courtly dance or dance song, a popular religious song, or a popular religious procession. The golden age of the English carol was about 1350–1550. The fifteenth-century carol is considered a masterpiece of English medieval music.

Carols disappeared almost completely when the Protestant Reformation arrived in the sixteenth century and the singing of biblical psalms arose to replace them. But the carol revived in the second half of the eighteenth century. About a hundred years later, E. Cuthbert Nunn (1868–1914) translated the French Renaissance carol "En Flambeau, Jeanette Isabella," into

47

English as "Bring a Torch, Jeanette, Isabella."

This is an upbeat song. Nothing about it is pompous. There is no formality here. Instead, it brings to mind the revels of a medieval Christmas parade. Townsfolk carry torches and sing as they proceed to the church to celebrate the nativity of Christ. They begin with a shout, "Bring a torch!" and a command, "Come swiftly and run!" But soon they fall into wonder at what has happened, "Ah, ah, how beautiful is the mother and her Son."

The folk of the village hurry, singing through the streets, hoping to see the Christ child. Then they slow to walk, catch their breath, and whisper as they enter the church, "Hush, hush! Peacefully now He sleeps."

O Christ,
bring a torch into my heart.
Warm it with Your love
and enlighten it
with Your truth.

Do You Hear What I Hear?

Said the shepherd boy to the mighty king,
Do you know what I know?
Is your palace warm, mighty king,
Do you know what I know?
A Child, a Child shivers in the cold;
Let us bring Him silver and gold,
Let us bring Him silver and gold.

NOEL REGNEY AND GLORIA SHAYNE

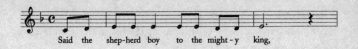

Said the shep-herd boy to the might-y king,

And suddenly
there was with the angel
a multitude of the heavenly host
praising God, and saying,
Glory to God in the highest,
and on earth peace,
good will toward men.
LUKE 2:13–14

In America, Christmas is an intense, busy time. Much of the nation's economic well-being depends upon the retail sales at this time of year. Children's toys are marketed as must-have items for Christmas morning. Hollywood turns out movies especially for the holiday season. Meanwhile, gatherings and parties in offices, homes, and communities feature special foods and the exchange of gifts, all amidst holiday decorations in abundance—holly, wreaths, evergreen trees, Santas, elves, reindeer, snowflakes, icicles, sleighs, bells, stars, and the like.

But if you are ever alone, all alone at this time of year, you may be able to hear the questions of Christmas. Questions like, "Do you see what I see?"

This is what the wise men asked the great leaders of Israel and the king of Judaea. But these men had not seen the star in the east.

Or you may hear the question that is the title of this Christmas song, "Do you hear what I hear?" The shepherds who heard the glorious angels announce the birth of Christ asked this question, "And all they that heard it wondered at those things which were told them by the shepherds" (Luke 2:18).

Mary, the mother of Jesus, "kept all these things, and pondered them in her heart" (verse 19). And so Mary might have asked another Christmas question, had she been so bold—"Do you know what I know?"

Jesus, I know You were
born long ago.
I know that Your life and death
changed the course of history.
Now, please let me know that
You are living in me.

O Come, All Ye Faithful

O come, all ye faithful, joyful and
   triumphant,
O come ye, O come ye, to Bethlehem.
Come and behold Him, born the King
   of angels;

Refrain

O come, let us adore Him,
O come, let us adore Him,
O come, let us adore Him,
Christ the Lord.

LATIN HYMN; ASCRIBED TO
JOHN FRANCIS WADE, C. 1711–1786

O come, all ye faith-ful, joy-ful and tri-um-phant, O

For God was pleased
to have all his fullness dwell in him,
and through him to reconcile to himself all things,
whether things on earth or things in heaven,
by making peace through his blood, shed on the cross.
COLOSSIANS 1:19–20 NIV

The hope given to humanity in the birth of Jesus Christ penetrates the entire world. That's why Christmas hymns come from so many sources. For example, "O Come, All Ye Faithful," sometimes called by its Latin title, *Adeste Fideles,* was written in Latin by an Englishman, John Francis Wade, who lived in France. Mr. Wade made his living transcribing sacred songs and other music into copy books that were used in church and family worship. His song invites the inhabitants of heaven and earth to greet their newly born king:

"*O come all ye, faithful*" is a call to the people living on earth.

"*Sing choirs of angels*" is a command to the beings of heaven.

In other words, the good news of the birth of Jesus Christ is for all creation. As the New Testament says:

Who is the image of the invisible God,
the firstborn of every creature:
For by him were all things created,
that are in heaven, and that are in earth,
visible and invisible, whether they be thrones,
or dominions, or principalities, or powers: all things
were created by him, and for him.
COLOSSIANS 1:15–16

This hymn sends an invitation out to every creature. Its last verse tells us how we should respond:

"Yea, Lord, we greet Thee." The Father's Word has appeared in flesh! *"O come, let us adore Him!"*

I thank You heavenly Father.
Your Word became flesh
and lived with us.
He was full of grace and truth.
Today I open my heart so
it can receive a little more
of the grace and truth
that is Your Son.

The Little Drummer Boy

Come they told me, pa rum pum pum pum,
A newborn King to see, pa rum pum pum
    pum,
Our finest gifts we bring, pa rum pum
    pum pum,
To lay before the King, pa rum pum pum pum
    rum pum pum pum rum pum pum pum,
So to honor Him, pa rum pum pum pum,
    when we come.

KATHERINE DAVIS,
HENRY ONORATI,
AND HARRY SIMEONE

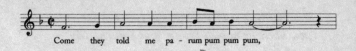

Come they told me pa - rum pum pum pum,

Praise him with the sound of the trumpet:
praise him with the psaltery and harp.
Praise him with the timbrel and dance:
praise him with stringed instruments and organs.
PSALM 150:3–4

An old man once told this story of how he came to live in Bethlehem:

> *I was born long ago in a land far away to the*
> *east of the sea. There I lived with my uncle, an*
> *astronomer. He was a wise man and knew every-*
> *thing there was to know about the stars—their*
> *names and the names of all the constellations and*
> *planets, when they would rise and set, and where*
> *they would be in the sky at all seasons. I spent*
> *many nights sitting on the rooftop with him long*
> *into the night. There Uncle and his companions*
> *taught me the legends of the heavenly lights.*
>
> *My uncle's house was high on a hilltop to the*
> *west of the city where nearly no one else lived.*
> *Once, on an early evening, I was on the roof qui-*
> *etly tapping on my drum,* pa rum pum pum pum,
> pa rum pum pum pum. *Uncle began to instruct*

me, pointing to two bright lights in the darkening sky. These he named Jupiter and Saturn. "My boy," he began, "this year, these two wandering stars will meet together three separate times and appear as a single bright star. Each time they unite, we will find them in the constellation Pisces—the constellation of the Jews who live in the hills of Israel near Jerusalem above the western sea." I knew of Jupiter, Saturn, and Pisces, but I had never before heard of the people called Jews.

"Jupiter is kingly and brings good fortune," Uncle said. "And Saturn portends wisdom. I believe that these two are joining to announce the birth of a wise King for Israel. Travelers from Jerusalem tell me that these have joined before as one star in Pisces. This occurred before the birth of another great Jewish leader, a prophet named Moses. I have studied to find if the Jewish Scripture mentions such a star. Indeed it does."

Uncle then drew a scroll out of a linen case. From it he read these words: "I see Him, but not now; I behold Him, but not near—a star shall come out of Jacob, and a scepter shall rise out of Israel." The soft silence of night came upon the rooftop as Uncle rerolled the scroll. Jupiter and Saturn slowly proceeded westerly across the blackened sky.

After a long while, clothing brushed and rustled, and Uncle and his companions arose from their places. "Come with us," they told me, "to see a newborn King. We will bring our finest gifts to

Him—gold, frankincense, and myrrh. These we will lay before the King when we come."

With Uncle and his companions, I followed the star, arriving here in Bethlehem when I was yet a boy. This, you see, is how I came to journey here from the east.

We found the King of the Jews in a small, unimpressive house where He lived with His mother, Mary, and His father, Joseph, a carpenter. The King was happily toddling about the well-swept earthen floor—not yet two years old. Joseph mentioned that the child's name was Jesus. My traveling companions all knelt in the little room where the boy was at play. I had never seen Uncle do such a thing before, so I got down on my knees, too.

Then we all went outside into the dooryard where Joseph kept the animals. The men found their three gifts amidst our baggage, gave them to Mary and Joseph for the boy, and we turned to leave. After a few steps I paused, turned back, and said, "Little Baby, I am a poor boy, too. I have no gift that's fit to give a King. Shall I play for You on my drum?"

Mary nodded and I began to softly tap, pa rum pum pum pum. *The ox and lamb kept time,* pa rum pum pum pum. *I played my drum for Him,* pa rum pum pum pum, pa rum pum pum pum. *I played my best for Him.* Pa rum pum pum pum, rum pum pum pum, rum pum pum pum. *Then He smiled at me; me and my drum.*

O GOD,
MAKE MY HEART SO SIMPLE
THAT I MAY WORSHIP YOUR SON
IN SPIRIT AND IN TRUTH.

Joy to the World!

Joy to the world, the Lord is come!
Let earth receive her King;
Let every heart prepare Him room,
And heaven and nature sing,
And heaven and nature sing,
And heaven, and heaven, and nature sing.

Isaac Watts, 1674–1748

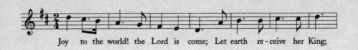

Joy to the world! the Lord is come; Let earth re-ceive her King;

Rejoice in the Lord always:
and again I say, Rejoice.
Let your moderation be known unto all men.
The Lord is at hand.
Philippians 4:4–5

In the days of Isaac Watts, the author of this hymn, there was in England extreme prejudice against newly-composed hymns. Congregations were strictly devoted to singing the Psalms in worship. So Watts reworked certain Psalms in freer and more spontaneous versions. In 1719, he published *Psalms of David, Imitated in the Language of the New Testament,* creating a new style of church music.

"Joy to the World" is based on Psalm 98, which tells of the Messiah's coming and kingdom. The reader may be able to see Watts's first stanza in Psalm 98:2–3—and the arrival of a victorious King. The second stanza is drawn from verses 4–8—through the praise of all creation. The fourth stanza is seen in verse 9—God's righteous and loving reign.

Watts strayed a little from Psalm 98 when he wrote the third stanza to this hymn—"No more let sins and sorrows grow/Nor thorns infest the ground." This seems to be a direct command from the divine King Himself. Then Watts returns to the psalm, imitating the last sentence in verse 3—"He comes to make His blessings flow/Far as the curse is found."

Set to a tune by the greatest of all English composers, George Friedrich Handel, "Joy to the World" can powerfully fill the heart with the joy of Christ's coming, especially when sung standing with a congregation on Christmas Eve!

LET EARTH RECEIVE HER KING.
LET HIM RULE THE WORLD
WITH TRUTH AND GRACE.
LET EVERY HEART PREPARE HIM ROOM.
LET THE NATIONS PROVE THE GLORIES
OF HIS RIGHTEOUSNESS
AND THE WONDERS OF HIS LOVE.
THANK YOU, LORD.

I Heard the Bells on Christmas Day

I heard the bells on Christmas day
Their old familiar carols play,
And wild and sweet the words repeat
Of peace on earth, good will to men.

HENRY W. LONGFELLOW, 1807–1882

I heard the bells on Christ-mas day Their

> *For he himself is our peace,*
> *who has made the two one*
> *and has destroyed the barrier,*
> *the dividing wall of hostility.*
> EPHESIANS 2:14 NIV

The lyrics to this song come from the beloved American poet Henry Wadsworth Longfellow. Perhaps the bells were those of the Episcopal seminary that is still active next door to the poet's historic home in Cambridge, Massachusetts.

Published in 1864, "I Heard the Bells on Christmas Day" sprang directly out of the cataclysmic American Civil War. So Longfellow mourns in the next-to-last stanza: "And in despair I bowed my head/'There is no peace on earth,' I said,/For hate is strong and mocks the song/Of peace on earth, good will to men."

But the bells answered him: "Then pealed the bells more loud and deep:/'God is not dead, nor doth he sleep;/ 'The wrong shall fail, the right prevail/With peace on earth, good will to men.' "

This is where most people believe the song ends. But Longfellow wrote two more stanzas that are omitted from hymnals. They tell of the battles then raging in the American South:

> *Then from each black, accursed mouth*
> *The cannon thundered in the South,*
> *And with the sound the carols drowned*
> *Of peace on earth, good will to men.*

> *It was as if an earthquake rent*
> *The hearth-stones of a continent,*
> *And made forlorn, the households born*
> *Of peace on earth, good will to men.*

Once the black, accursed mouths of cannon thundered in our country. Today civil, religious, and international wars make households forlorn in many nations—especially in Africa. Let us pray for the people of these households this Christmas. Pray that it will also come to others.

Jesus Christ, You said,
"Blessed are those who mourn,
for they will be comforted."
I mourn for the people
who are suffering
in this war-torn world.
Extend Your great mercy to them,
and bring peace to that place.

Silent Night

Silent night, holy night,
All is calm, all is bright
Round yon virgin mother and Child.
Holy Infant, so tender and mild,
Sleep in heavenly peace,
Sleep in heavenly peace.

JOSEPH MOHR, 1792–1848

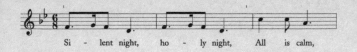

Si - lent night, ho - ly night, All is calm,

And there were in the same country
shepherds abiding in the field,
keeping watch over their flock by night.
LUKE 2:8

Sometime in January 1819, Karl Mauracher of Zillerthal, Austria, came to St. Nicholas Church in Oberndorf to repair the church's organ. While he was there, the assistant priest of the church, Joseph Mohr, and its acting organist, Franz Grüber, taught him a song they had recently written: "Silent Night."

The organ at St. Nicholas Church had broken shortly before Christmas. Without an organ, what would the church do for music on Christmas Eve? Mohr and Grüber rose to the occasion: Mohr wrote eighteen short, simple, poetic lines, and Grüber set them to music for two voices, choir, and guitar. So "Silent Night" came to be. If Mr. Mauracher had been available to repair the organ earlier, the world's best-known Christmas carol may never have been written.

In the following years, Karl Mauracher spread the song throughout the Tyrolean region of western Austria. Yet the music to "Silent Night" was not published until

1840 among "Four Genuine Tyrolean Songs, Sung by the Strasser Sisters from Zillerthal." Tyrolean songs and singers were popular music hall attractions throughout Europe and America in those days. The song was widely sung.

Today, "Silent Night" is still sung everywhere people gather to remember the birth of Jesus Christ. The images of the song infuse memories of Christmas Eve like fragrant tea in a warm cup—the holy night when all is calm and bright; the holy infant, tender and mild, sleeping in heavenly peace; the angels singing, "Christ the Savior is born."

"Silent Night" is such a simple song, yet an unforgettable one—because it makes known the dawn of redeeming grace, the profound birth of Jesus Christ.

Almighty God,
I am in awe of Your ways.
Thank You that You sent
my Redeemer to that
little middle-eastern town
on that silent night so long ago!

O Holy Night!

O holy night, the stars are brightly shining;
It is the night of the dear Savior's birth!
Long lay the world in sin and error pining,
Till He appeared and the soul felt its worth.
A thrill of hope, the weary soul rejoices,
For yonder breaks a new and glorious morn.

Refrain

Fall on your knees, O hear the angel voices!
O night divine, O night when Christ was born!
O night, O holy night, O night divine!

PLACIDE CLAPPEAU

O ho-ly night! the stars are bright-ly

*Thou shalt love the Lord thy God
with all thy heart,
and with all thy soul,
and with all thy mind.
Thou shalt love thy neighbour as thyself.
On these two commandments hang
all the law and the prophets.*
MATTHEW 22:37, 39–40

This gentle song was written in 1847 by Placide Clappeau, a wine merchant and mayor of Roquemaure, France, who wrote poems for his own enjoyment. It says that, at Christmas, one can be "led by the light of faith serenely beaming," to stand with a glowing heart by Christ's cradle.

The song continues, "So led by light of a star sweetly gleaming,/Here came the wise men from Orient land." Did you know that, using only your eyes, you can see about two thousand stars on a clear, dark night? Among all the stars, all the attractions of the holiday season, look for the star of faith. If you follow it, you'll find "the King of kings lay thus in lowly manger,/In all our trials born to be our friend!"

Christ's gospel is ruled by a single, new commandment "That ye love one another; as I have loved you" (John 13:34). So the final verse to "O Holy Night" begins: "Truly He taught us to love one another."

In what way did Jesus teach us to love one another? Was it enough for Him to simply say it? To command it? "Thou shalt love one another." No, this is not what He did. He taught by example, and His birth is the world's first lesson in love. The Gospel of John explains, "For God so loved the world, that he gave his only begotten Son, that whosoever believeth in him should not perish, but have everlasting life. For God sent not his Son into the world to condemn the world; but that the world through him might be saved" (John 3:16–17).

I worship You, O God,
that You did not send the Son
into the world to
condemn the world,
but that the world
might be saved through Him.
Thank You so much.

Let There Be Peace on Earth

Let there be peace on earth
And let it begin with me;
Let there be peace on earth,
The peace that was meant to be.
With God as our Father,
Brothers all are we.
Let me walk with my brother
In perfect harmony.
Let peace begin with me,
Let this be the moment now.
With every step I take,
Let this be my solemn vow;
To take each moment and live each
    moment in peace eternally.
Let there be peace on earch and let it
    begin with me.

JILL JACKSON

Let there be peace on earth And let it be - gin with

Peace I leave with you,
my peace I give unto you.
JOHN 14:27

The Christmas season can cause many emotions and desires to arise in a person's soul. Some of these feelings are good and others bad. The drive for satisfaction in material things, for example, is negative. Those who have gone down that path and returned report that it ends in grief. On the other hand, the sentiment of the song "Let There Be Peace on earth" is positive. It's not an easy thing to, as the song says, "let it begin with me," but the value of peaceful living is inestimable.

The New Testament tells the story of how one can be a source of peace on earth. The story begins with God's love in sending the Son to live among us. It goes on to tell of Christ's love in dying to settle the controversy between God and humanity. After this came the ultimate act of love—the resurrection of Jesus Christ—a victorious event that smashed the power of death beyond repair. It also released the Holy Spirit to live within the human race and personally bring the love of God into the heart of anyone who will believe.

This astonishing story reaches its zenith in the lives of ordinary people who, by faith, allow the Spirit to make a home in their hearts. This empowers people to live lives of love. Here is a description of such a life:

Love is patient, love is kind.
It does not envy, it does not boast,
it is not proud.
It is not rude, it is not self-seeking,
it is not easily angered,
it keeps no record of wrongs.
Love does not delight in evil
but rejoices with the truth.
It always protects, always trusts,
always hopes, always perseveres.
1 CORINTHIANS 13:4–7 NIV

I bow my knees, Father,
to pray that You
would strengthen me
in my inner being with power
through Your Spirit.
And that Christ may dwell
in my heart through faith,
as I am being rooted
and grounded in love.

Lo! How a Rose E'er Blooming

Lo, how a Rose e'er blooming from tender
    stem hath sprung!
Of Jesse's lineage coming, as those of old
    have sung.
It came, a floweret bright, amid the cold
    of winter,
When half spent was the night.
Isaiah 'twas foretold it, the Rose I have in
    mind;
With Mary we behold it, the virgin
    mother kind.
To show God's love aright, she bore to us
    a Savior,
When half spent was the night.
The shepherds heard the story proclaimed
    by angels bright,
How Christ, the Lord of glory was born
    on earth this night.
To Bethlehem they sped and in the manger
    they found Him,
As angel heralds said.
This Flower, whose fragrance tender with
    sweetness fills the air,
Dispels with glorious splendor the darkness
    everywhere;
True Man, yet very God, from sin and

death He saves us,
And lightens every load.
O Savior, Child of Mary, Who felt our
human woe,
O Savior, King of glory, Who dost our
weakness know;
Bring us at length we pray, to the bright
courts of heaven,
And to the endless day!

GERMAN CAROL, 16TH CENTURY

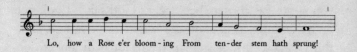

Lo, how a Rose e'er bloom-ing From ten-der stem hath sprung!

And in that day there shall be a root of Jesse,
which shall stand for an ensign of the people;
to it shall the Gentiles seek:
and his rest shall be glorious.
ISAIAH 11:10

This song was first published in 1588 as "Es Ist ein Ros' Entsprungen," a medieval Christmas carol. It originally had twenty-three stanzas, each comparing Mary to a rose. This idea came from a mystical rose tradition associated with a verse in the Song of Solomon, "I am the rose of Sharon" (2:1).

When the Reformation rolled across Europe, the song was revised for use by Protestants. In the new version, Mary became the rose bush that bore the true Rose, Jesus Christ. The song's first verse mixes its metaphors and alludes to Isaiah 11:1, "And there shall come forth a rod out of the stem of Jesse, and a Branch shall grow out of his roots." This is Christ.

You may be wondering, "Who is this fellow, Jesse?"

Jesse, the father of David, first appears in the Bible in 1 Samuel 16. He had eight sons, seven of whom were rejected as the choice for king of Israel. David, the youngest, was chosen, because, as God said, "Look not on his countenance, or on the height of his stature. . .for the LORD seeth not as man seeth; for man looketh on the outward appearance, but the LORD looketh on the heart" (verse 7).

Eventually, David's kingdom was cut down like a tree, leaving behind the stump of Jesse. About thirty generations after David, Jesus was born as King of the Jews. This is why we now sing about Christ as the shoot who came out of the stump of Jesse.

Oh! Jesus,
sweetly scented Rose,
through Your believers,
spread in every place
the fragrance that comes from knowing You.
Make us the aroma
of Christ
among all people.

Good King Wenceslas

Good King Wenceslas looked out on
    the Feast of Stephen,
When the snow lay round about,
    deep and crisp and even.
Brightly shone the moon that night,
    though the frost was cruel,
When a poor man came in sight,
    gathering winter fuel.

JOHN M. NEALE

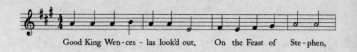

Good King Wen - ces - las look'd out,   On the Feast of   Ste - phen,

And let us not be weary in well doing:
for in due season we shall reap, if we faint not.
As we have therefore opportunity,
let us do good unto all men, especially unto them
who are of the household of faith.
GALATIANS 6:9–10

To set the scene for this Christmas carol, let's first answer two questions: First, who was Wenceslas? And what is the feast of Stephen?

Wenceslas was the Duke of Bohemia during the early tenth century. Bohemia is now a region in the western Czech Republic. Wenceslas converted to the Christian faith and encouraged Bohemia's turn to Christianity. St. Stephen's day is a religious feast observed on December 26. It commemorates the first Christian martyr.

So, the curtain rises on King Wenceslas in Eastern Europe, late in December sometime before 920 A.D., looking out his window at the moonlit, snow-covered landscape. He catches sight of a poor man, struggling through the deep snow and bitter cold, collecting firewood. This begins an allegorical story. Its characters and events symbolically express a deeper meaning.

Wenceslas represents God. He leaves his warm home to provide for the poor man's needs, just as God came to earth as Jesus Christ to seek and to save the lost. The page, or servant, who follows Wenceslas, symbolizes a believer in Christ. As he follows his Lord in the wintry, cold world, he begins to falter, "Fails my heart, I know not how;" he cries, "I can go no longer."

"Mark my footsteps," says the king, "tread thou in them boldly." The servant does so and finds he can more easily follow.

"Good King Wenceslas" was written and published in 1853 by the Englishman J. M. Neale, perhaps to encourage people to follow in the charitable footsteps of the Master where, "Ye who now will bless the poor, shall yourselves find blessing."

GRACIOUS GOD,
EXTEND CHARITY BEYOND
THIS CHARITABLE SEASON.
CAUSE ME TO WALK IN
YOUR FOOTSTEPS
AND IN THE FOOTSTEPS
OF THOSE WHO FIRST
FOLLOWED YOU,
WHO WERE EAGER
TO REMEMBER THE POOR.

WE WISH YOU A MERRY CHRISTMAS

We wish you a Merry Christmas;
We wish you a Merry Christmas;

We wish you a Merry Christmas and a
Happy New Year.

Good tidings we bring to you and your kin;

Good tidings for Christmas and a Happy
New Year.

TRADITIONAL

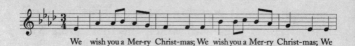

We wish you a Mer-ry Christ-mas; We wish you a Mer-ry Christ-mas; We

Is any merry?
let him sing psalms.
JAMES 5:13

In 1822, Davies Gilbert published in England the first modern collection of traditional carols. He saw them as belonging to a past world that had all but disappeared. Here is how Gilbert described what happened on Christmas Eve in the "Protestant West of England" through the late eighteenth century: "At seven or eight o'clock in the evening cakes were drawn hot from the oven; cider or beer exhilarated the spirits in every house; and the singing of Carols was continued late into the night. On Christmas Day these Carols took the place of Psalms in all the churches, especially at afternoon service, the whole congregation joining; and at the end it was usual for the Parish Clerk to declare, in a loud voice, his wishes for a merry Christmas and a happy New Year to all the parishioners."

"We Wish You a Merry Christmas" comes out of the English country tradition of wassailers who went from door to door singing and drinking to the health of those they visited. This practice goes far back to medieval times. It probably had pre-Christian origins in the fertility rites with which the first carols were associated. In the cities of England, wassailing merged with the tradition of "waits," or watchmen, who went through the streets sounding a horn or crying out to mark the passing hours of the night. So the term "waits" became a word for parties of singers and musicians who went from house to house at Christmastime. A book titled *Popular Antiquities* (1795) noted that in Newcastle upon Tyne and other places in the North of England, boys and girls went round on the nights leading up to Christmas, including Christmas Eve, "knocking at the doors and singing their Christmas Carols."

Caroling—a joyous, ancient tradition worthy of revival in the twenty-first century.

O Christ, O gift of God.
Save me from judging my joy
by the number of pretty packages
found under a pretty tree.
I pray for the gift
of song so that I can sing
and make melody
in my heart to You.

Inspirational Library

Beautiful purse/pocket-size editions of Christian classics bound in flexible leatherette. These books make thoughtful gifts for everyone on your list, including yourself!

When I'm on My Knees　　The highly popular collection of devotional thoughts on prayer, especially for women.
　　Flexible Leatherette. $4.99

The Bible Promise Book　　Over 1,000 promises from God's Word arranged by topic. What does God promise about matters like: Anger, Illness, Jealousy, Love, Money, Old Age, and Mercy? Find out in this book!
　　Flexible Leatherette. $3.99

Daily Wisdom for Women　　A daily devotional for women seeking biblical wisdom to apply to their lives. Scripture taken from the New American Standard Version of the Bible.
　　Flexible Leatherette. $4.99

My Daily Prayer Journal　　Each page is dated and features a Scripture verse and ample room for you to record your thoughts, prayers, and praises. One page for each day of the year.
　　Flexible Leatherette. $4.99

Available wherever books are sold.
Or order from:

Barbour Publishing, Inc.
P.O. Box 719
Uhrichsville, OH 44683
www.barbourbooks.com

If you order by mail, add $2.00 to your order for shipping.
Prices are subject to change without notice.